Busy Mom's Guide to Working Online

"50 Smart Ways to Make Money Online From The Comfort of Your Home."

Copyright © [2024 by [Beatrice W. N]

All rights reserved.

No portion of this book may be reproduced in any form without written permission from the publisher or author, except as permitted by the copyright law.

Busy Mom's Guide to Working Online

"50 Smart Ways to Make Money Online: Step by Step Guide for Beginners."

- Preface
- Introduction
- Chapter 1: Basics of Working Online
    - What Working Online Entails
    - Is Working Online For You?
    - What do you need to start working online?
    - 12 Benefits of Working Online
    - 7 Cons Of Working Online
- CHAPTER 2: How to Get Started
    - Potential Income: Can You Earn A Living Working Online?
    - 15 High-Income Skills You Should Learn
    - 10 Tips for Finding Work Online
    - 10 Habits That Hold You Back from Achieving Your Dream of Working Online and How to Stop Them
    - 20 Ways to Improve Your Earning Potential
    - Top 8 Secrets of Successful People Who Work Online
- Chapter 3: 50 Smart Ways to Make Money Online for Beginners
    1. Become a Freelancer
    2. Writing Articles on Authority Websites
    3. Become a Ghostwriter
    4. Sell your Service on Fiverr
    5. Start a blog
    6. Sell Quote Printables
    7. Creating Niche Websites
    8. Become a Proofreader
    9. Start a Dropshipping Business
    10. Pinterest Marketing
    11. Become a Social Media Evaluator
    12. Start Data Entry Work
    13. Sell Crafts and Art on Etsy
    14. Becoming an Amazon Associate
    15. Reselling Items on eBay
    16. Become a Virtual Call Centre agent
    17. Instagram Marketing
    18. Write Taglines and Slogans
    19. Do Graphic Design
    20. Publishing a Kindle eBook
    21. Do Interview Transcribing
    22. Sell video course on Udemy.com

23. Create a Membership site
24. Creating and Editing Videos
25. Starting a YouTube Channel
26. Start Copywriting
27. Join Appen.com
28. Sell Private Label Rights (PLR)
29. Do Affiliate Marketing
30. Becoming an Online Tutor
31. Doing Document Translation
32. Becoming a Research Assistant
33. Become a Social Media Manager
34. Do Voice Acting (Voice Overs)
35. Sell products or services online
36. Join Q&A Sites
37. Starting your Book Review Store
38. Click and Sell photos
39. Get Paid to Tweet
40. Do Email Marketing
41. Become a Captioner
42. Sell Products on Zazzle
43. Start Your Podcast
44. Doing Smartphone Photography
45. Do Facebook Marketing
46. Join Focus Groups
47. Joining Micro Job Sites
48. Sell Print on Demand Products
49. Share Links on Social Media
50. Buy and Sell Domain Names

Chapter 4: BONUS
    Bonus 1: 20 Best Job Boards to Find Remote Work
    Bonus 2: 60 FAQS About Working Online

Conclusion

Preface

Welcome to "Busy Mom's Guide to Working Online: 50 Smart Ways to Make Money Online" - the ultimate guide for anyone looking to make money from the comfort of their own home.

Are you tired of the 9-5 grind and want to explore other options for making a living? Do you dream of having the freedom to work from anywhere in the world? Then this comprehensive guide is perfect for you!

The book is designed to give you a comprehensive guide on how to make money online through 50 legitimate and proven methods. From freelancing and virtual assistance to affiliate marketing and e-commerce, we cover it all. You'll discover how to turn your skills and passions into a profitable online business.

This book is perfect for beginners who have no idea where to start. We provide you with all the resources and tools you need to succeed in the online world. You'll learn the most effective ways to find work, get paid, and grow your income. Whether you're a stay-at-home mom, a recent graduate, or anyone looking to escape the traditional 9-5 work routine, our course is designed to help you achieve your financial goals.

In addition to our 50 ways of making money online, the book includes bonus resources like links to books, courses, or sites where you can learn more about each method to help you launch your online career and start earning money right away.

The book is designed for individuals who are interested in starting a career or supplementing their income through online work. With the rise of remote work and the gig economy, there has never been a better time to explore the opportunities available for making money online.

The book will be super helpful for moms who wish to utilize their skills to work online and have time and location freedom. However, it is still helpful for everyone who wishes to get ideas of legitimate ways to work online.

Introduction

In the current economic crisis, it is necessary for both parents to work for a liveable income. Yet, getting back to work after having a baby is one of the greatest struggles for women. The continued motherhood penalty and pregnancy bias in the workplace are some of the reasons why women decide to start working online. Working from home offers a flexible schedule to make appointments and saves you from the anxiety of leaving your baby in someone else's care.

I share the tips in this book as a mother who had to make tough choices after going back to work after maternity leave. It was tough in the initial years, balancing work and motherhood. And one day I was forced to choose work or my child who was unwell. I know you know the choice I made!

Throughout the book, you will also receive practical advice and guidance on how to build a successful online business, how to effectively monetize your skills and online brand, as well as access to resources and tools to help you along the way.

By the end of this book, you will have a solid understanding of what working online entails, the top ways to make money online, and beginner steps to get started. You will get a wealth of resources and strategies to help you get there. You will learn the essential skills and strategies needed to succeed online, such as marketing your services, finding clients, and creating a strong online presence.

Whether you're a beginner or have some experience with online work, this book is the perfect way to learn how to take your skills to the next level and start earning money from the comfort of your own home. So, come and join us on this exciting journey!

So let's get started!

Chapter 1: Basics of Working Online

What Working Online Entails

Working online (remotely) is a job situation millions of workers dream of. The internet is a low-cost field enabling people to make money online. However, many scams online make finding work online harder than it should be. Avoid getting scammed; do not pay for the privilege. Like any other job, working online requires effort and perseverance.

Here is a starting point for working online

1. Self-reflection

- What are you passionate about?
- What are your abilities?
- Do you have a career?
- Do you want to do something new?

You are not limited to one job. Having various career ideas increases your possibilities.

When you choose to work online, it is also important to consider your intention.

- Do you want to make ends meet?
- Are you trying to meet people for more adult time?
- Are you embarking on your career?

Your motive will help you narrow down on the most suitable career options for you.

2. Availability

There are both full-time and part-time online jobs offering from 5 to more than 40 hours weekly. See what your childcare schedule is and find a job that fits.

- How much time are you willing to invest in your online job?
- Are you only available on weekends or weekdays?

Knowing what you need will save you so much time.

3. **Research**

There are thousands of legitimate companies offering telecommuting jobs. Talk to your professional and social network for recommendations. You can also create a profile on LinkedIn and back it up with your online network. It is important to have a support system during your job search and after you start working online.

4. **Connect With Other Working Mums**

Social media has made it possible to interact with people in similar situations. Join a working mums group and get to know their challenges and experiences. This will help you learn new tricks and prevent you from making common mistakes. When you speak to people who are familiar with the process, you will get an insight into how to plot your working plan.

5. **Stay Woke**

The internet is loaded with scam jobs. Enticing job listings promising high returns for easy work are red flags. Most of these scam jobs do not identify the name of the hiring company and use public email domains such as @gmail.com, @hotmail.com, or anonymous @craigslist.com.

Be careful of what you key in on to search for online jobs. "Work at home" has been identified as one of the riskiest keywords and a common scam. Use safer words like "telecommuting "or "remote work." If you think the deal is too good, then think twice and do some more research.

6. **What Are Your Skills?**

Focus on your professional persona. Translate your mom time into skills like organization, time management, decision making, and leadership. Give yourself time to reconnect with your professional self. It is not easy to switch to the professional you are after playing the parenting role for so long.

7. **Make A Plan**

It is advisable to start small. Try several days a week and see how it goes. You need to set priorities to achieve a balance. Some of the things to consider include:

- **Childcare-** What kind and how much childcare do you need?
- **Home office-** You need a place within the house, with minimal distractions, to set up your office
- **Ground rules-** It can be difficult to adjust to working at home for you and your family. It is important to make rules and expectations for an easier transition.
- **Save-** As you start up, you will likely have a lower income. Build a nest egg to avoid financial strains.
- **Organization-** For maximum productivity, put things in place to organize your work life and home life for things to run smoothly.

Is Working Online For You?

Working online from home is not for everyone. Some mums need more separation between their professional and personal lives. Others get satisfaction when everything that matters to them is within their reach. Working online has pros and cons, but for most mums, the benefits outweigh the drawbacks.

There are a few requirements for mums working from home. For instance, your family needs should be considered before you start your work-from-home job. Ensure you choose something that you enjoy doing and works for the whole family. Here are some things that can help you determine if working online is for you.

- **Childcare**

You may not need a babysitter if you plan to work around your child's schedule. However, if you will work more hours or get a full-time remote job, you may need to plan how to get child care services.

Do you have a good support network of a home personal assistant or babysitter? Some mums have spouses who can take charge on weekends or evenings. Some kids require extra care, depending on their needs.

See if your level of flexibility will meet the demands of your online job. Do you find it hard to say no? It is not the best experience having family responsibilities taking up your work time or feeling like you have to work all the time

• **Distractions**

Even with full-time childcare, it is almost inevitable to deal with distractions. Unlike in regular offices, home distractions are personal. Motherly instincts might urge you to offer comfort even with the presence of your childcare provider.

- **Skills and Experience**

You may be well-suited for working online if you have skills or experience that can be applied to online work, such as writing, graphic design, programming, or customer service.

Online work often requires a basic understanding of technology and an ability to use various online tools and platforms. If you are starting an online business or a new online job, you might have to brush up your skills or complete a short course ahead of time. You will be more confident to get started.

- **Flexibility**

Online work offers greater flexibility than traditional jobs, allowing you to set your hours, work from anywhere with an internet connection, and balance work with other commitments. Working online often requires a high level of self-discipline and motivation, as you may not have a boss or colleagues to hold you accountable.

- **Work style**

Some people thrive in an environment where they can work independently, while others prefer the structure and social interaction of a traditional workplace.

Ultimately, the best way to determine if working online is right for you is to try it out and see how it feels. Start by exploring different online work opportunities and see if you enjoy the work and find it fulfilling.

What do you need to start working online?

Having the right equipment and resources is important to help you be more productive and efficient and make the most of the opportunities available.

Here's what you need to start working online:

1. A reliable computer and internet connection

A computer with a fast internet connection is essential for most online work. Invest in a quality computer and high-speed internet that can meet your needs and support the type of work you plan to do.

2. A comfortable workspace

Setting up a comfortable and ergonomic workspace is important for physical and mental health. Consider factors such as lighting, temperature, and ergonomic equipment, such as a chair and desk.

3. Productivity tools

There are various productivity tools and software programs available to help you manage your work and stay organized. Consider tools like project management software, time-tracking apps, and cloud storage services to help streamline your workflow.

4. Online marketing and networking tools

Building your online presence and connecting with potential clients and collaborators is key to success in the online marketplace. Consider using social media platforms, such as LinkedIn and Twitter, to network and promote your work.

5. A professional portfolio

Your portfolio is your calling card and showcases your skills and experience to potential clients. Invest time and effort in building a strong, professional portfolio that showcases your best work.

6. A payment processing solution

To receive payments from clients, you'll need a secure and reliable payment processing solution, such as PayPal, Wise, Stripe or a payment processor that integrates with your website or online platform.

7. Support system

Working online can be isolating, and it's important to have a support system in place. Consider joining online communities or groups, reaching out to other online workers for advice and support, and maintaining regular communication with family and friends.

12 Benefits of Working Online

Working online can offer numerous benefits and provide a fulfilling and lucrative career for self-motivated people who can work independently. Here are some of the benefits:

1. Better work-life balance for moms

With the flexibility to work from home or anywhere, you may have a better work-life balance than a traditional job.

Working online allows you to take part in your kid's daily routine. You get to spend your breaks with your young ones and hear what your children have been up to. When working online, you have no time limitation with your kids and can always work around their schedules.

2. Maintain or increase your income

If you left your career to raise kids, working online is a great way to return into the workforce. You will still have the privilege of parenting hands-on while you make some money. Many online work opportunities offer competitive pay, and you may be able to earn more than you would in a traditional job.

3. No more commute

Commuting can be time consuming and expensive. Working online eliminates commuting, creating more time with family and work. You can save money on car insurance, gas, or public transportation. Working online eliminates the need for a daily commute, saving time and money and reducing your carbon footprint.

4. Flexible work hours

One of the biggest benefits of working online is the ability to set your schedule and work from anywhere with an internet connection. This allows you to balance work with other commitments, such as family, travel, or other interests.

You have complete control over your schedule. You can choose to work after the kids go to bed or early in the morning.

5. It gives a feeling of contentment

Working online makes time for you. You feel in control of your life. You can comfortably balance your work life and family life. Depending on your work input, you can control your income and enjoy luxuries you could otherwise have forgo.

6. Saving on childcare expenses

Depending on the work and the children's age, some moms do not need to get outside childcare. Based on the type of childcare and how much, you can adjust your budget if you work part-time.

7. Forget the office dynamics

In the office environment, your decisions are mostly influenced by co-workers. You have to acknowledge your colleagues from time to time. When working online, you escape the frequent distractions of unscheduled chats in the washroom, unnecessary meetings, and social gatherings. You can comfortably delay responding to phone calls and emails. However, some mums might crave the social aspect of the office.

8. More savings

You will probably spend less on lunch and work clothes. However, working in pajamas, especially with kids at home, is not recommended. They look up to you as a role model.

9. Better lifestyle

Moms who work online have more time to exercise. You can finally volunteer in the community. You have more time to cook a healthy dinner for your family. You can book the next flight to Hawaii without the hassle of taking days off work. When working online, you can attain a healthier and happier lifestyle.

10. Independence

Kids learn to be independent when their mom is not available all day long. They have no alternative option but to pack their bags, prepare uniforms, and do their homework. These little tasks make a child more responsible and independent.

11. Better living standards

Working online offers better financial outcomes since you can work for more than one employer on a freelance basis. You want your family to live a comfortable and healthy life. Your kids do not have to miss out on all the pleasures children enjoy today.

12. Career advancement

Online work provides opportunities for ongoing learning and career development, as you can take on new projects, learn new skills, and grow your business. Online work allows you to connect with clients and customers from all over the world, expanding your potential market and increasing your earning potential.

7 Cons Of Working Online

While working online has many benefits, it does have potential drawbacks. It's important to weigh the pros and cons carefully and determine if working online is right for you, taking into account your personal circumstances, skills, and preferences. By understanding the potential challenges and developing a solid strategy, you can maximize opportunities and succeed as an online worker.

Here are a few cons to keep in mind:

1. Isolation

Working from home or from remote locations can lead to feelings of isolation and loneliness, especially if you miss the social interaction of a traditional workplace.

Even if you are not home alone, an adult company is sometimes much needed. You lack different perspectives from co-workers. If you are working with a remote team, consider team retreats at least once every year. You can also be part of an internal blog where moms working online publish their daily achievements and encounters.

2. Difficult communication

You no longer have your colleague beside you for those quick questions. When working remotely, you might require documenting every conversation. You must balance overwhelming communication streams, including emails, instant messaging apps, and video call software. It is very easy to miss important information.

3. Loss of productivity

When working from home, it can be challenging to maintain focus and avoid distractions, such as household chores, television, or social media.

From playing with the toddler to after lunch naps, many distractions can take up the time you should be working. A task that can take 2 hours while working from an office can take 5 hours while working from home.

Without the structure and routine of a traditional job, it can be difficult to stay motivated and on track, especially if you lack self-discipline.

4. Bad eating habits

A full refrigerator and kids eating all day are an effortless way to acquire bad eating habits. When working online, it is easy for mums to neglect self-care. Consider having healthy snacks and exercising regularly.

5. Quantity over quality

Working from home will be an adjustment for your kids as well. Being around them all day does not automatically mean you are available. Engage in your children's activities and share their enthusiasm.

6. Unreliable income:

Depending on the type of online work you do, your income may fluctuate and may not be as reliable as a traditional job with a steady salary. The online marketplace is highly competitive, and you may find it difficult to stand out and find clients, especially if you're starting from scratch.

7. Career advancement

If you decide to telecommute at your current job, you risk missing a promotion. Some of the unsupportive management translates working online into a lack of commitment.

These are some of the cons that may affect working online. However, the benefits of working online do outweigh the cons. In the next chapter, we will look into how to get started working online.

CHAPTER 2: How to Get Started

Potential Income: Can You Earn A Living Working Online?

Working online offers the flexibility and convenience of working from home or anywhere with an internet connection. But one of the biggest questions on everyone's mind is, "Can I actually earn a living working online?" The short answer is yes, you can, but the reality is more complex.

The amount of money you can earn working online depends on several factors, including your skills, experience, and the type of work you do. For example, freelance writing, graphic design, and programming can offer high-paying opportunities, while more entry-level jobs, such as data entry or customer service, may offer lower pay.

However, with the right approach and strategy, it is possible to build a successful and lucrative career working online.

Here are a few tips to help you increase your earning potential:

1. Specialize in a niche: By focusing on a specific area of expertise, you can become a sought-after specialist and command higher fees for your work.
2. Build a strong portfolio: Your portfolio is your calling card and showcases your skills and experience to potential clients. Invest time and effort in building a strong, professional portfolio that showcases your best work.
3. Network and market yourself: Networking and marketing are key to finding new clients and opportunities. Attend online events, join online communities, and use social media and other platforms to promote your work, keep up with the latest trends, and connect with potential clients.
4. Keep learning and expanding your skills: To stay competitive and increase your earning potential, it's important to keep learning and expanding your skills. Consider taking online courses, attending workshops, or pursuing further education in your field.
5. Be willing to invest in yourself: Investing in yourself, such as by purchasing equipment, software, courses or coaching can help you improve your work, increase your earning potential, and achieve financial stability.

15 High-Income Skills You Should Learn

Working online can earn you a living, depending on your skill. Legit online jobs are on the rise as the internet continues to grow. In most cases, the input and the risk you take determine the reward. The good news is it all takes organization, focus, and self-discipline, which is within your control.

Moms require online jobs that accommodate a busy lifestyle.

Here are some online jobs that need minimal schooling and zero start-up capital.

- Virtual assistant
- Social media marketing
- SEO specialist
- Blogging
- Affiliate marketing
- Web development
- Photography
- Video editing
- Resume writing
- Renting out space (Air BNB)
- Transcription
- Customer service representative
- Creating and selling an online course
- Online tutor
- Proofreading

These 15 online jobs or ways to earn online are always on demand. In the next chapter, we will go into detail about all the above.

10 Tips for Finding Work Online

The biggest concern about working online for most people is the fear of being scammed. The truth is, for every single legitimate online job, there are more than 50 scam jobs. If you follow the right steps, you can work online without ever getting scammed right from the beginning. So, how do you land an online job? Here are important tips to use.

1. Familiarize yourself with the online job boards

When it comes to working online, you can either start your business or join an existing company. These tips apply to the latter. The first step is to find companies that hire remote workers. There are companies that specifically advertise jobs for remote workers. For example, Flexjobs, Problogger, Outsourcely, Remotive, and Weworkremotely are good starting points. They offer remote startups and numerous jobs to choose from.

Most companies offering online jobs often advertise job postings in general job directories. If you do extensive research, you can always hunt them down. Make a shortlist of remote companies on a spreadsheet. See if their content is your match. Are they planning to launch products soon? Learn their language before sending out an application.

2. Hone the required skills

Now that you know the players, what can you offer? There are both tech and non-tech jobs in the online world. To find the skill you should focus on, reflect on:

- What do you love to do?
- What are you good at?
- What are people willing to pay for?

Do you have transferable soft skills?

Even with undeveloped skills, good soft skills can give you a chance of getting an online job as long as you can build upon technical skills. If you know of a team that works online, see if you can join them for exposure. Then, learn as you grow.

3. Build a strong online presence

In most cases, you might never meet your online employer in real life. It is easier to get a job if your potential employer likes you even before the first Skype interview. You need to build your personal brand. What is the search result if you Google your name?

Let your employers have a picture of your personality and skills. Discuss projects you are working on, on a blog. Exude passion and expertise for things that matter to you. Showcase the progress of a skill you are learning.

If you are not into blogging, utilize social media. Follow remote companies on social media. They will always make an update when they are growing their team.

4. Be proactive

With confidence in your skills and profile, you can start applying for work. The online world is highly competitive. To stand out, you require more than just a CV.

You can't just apply and wait. Think of ways you can leverage your network. Referrals are extremely effective. Use online platforms like LinkedIn to spot any connection with your potential boss.

Do you know anyone working in the job you are eyeing? They might have led to similar hiring positions. Don't be shy to send out personal messages. You may get noticed. Ensure your messages prove you can be of added value to your potential employer.

Understanding the team's challenges and objectives will help you find the right words to describe what you will do for the company. When you reach out, you increase your chances of getting the job.

5. Use your existing network

Do you know any business owners in your community? Offer them your services as the start of your online career. Let your network know you are in search of an online job. Post up on your social media.

6. **Connect with other freelancers**

It is easy to find freelancers on freelance Facebook or Reddit groups. During your online career, you might come across jobs your skills do not fit. It happens to other freelancers as well.

When you connect with them, you can easily share the available opportunities. Local co-working spaces and social media groups are other venues to connect with freelancers.

7. **Identify ideal platforms for your services**

Various websites allow you to self-advertise so that clients can contact you. Others allow you to find specific industries and types of work. You don't have to do the overwhelming online search. Here are 5 popular freelancing platforms:

•**Freelancer**

Freelancer hosts more than 8 million online projects in various categories. There is no membership fee required to access the project listings.

- **Upwork**

Upwork is largely recognized for remote work. You only need to submit a proposal when a project matches your skill or interests you. Clients often receive hundreds of proposals to choose from, so ensure that your portfolio stands out.

- **Fiverr**

From bookkeeping to data entry, Fiverr links freelancers with clients looking for various services such as logo design, email newsletters, writing, or web design. The site is recommendable for those offering quick projects or freelancers who are starting out

- **FreeeUp**

Freeeup vets freelancers skilled in web development, marketing, virtual assistance, and ecommerce customer service representatives, among others. Once approved, it is easy to land yourself a remote job. You don't need to apply or bid. FreeeUp fills requests within 48 hours.

- **TopTal**

Even with the thorough screening for freelancers, TopTal is one of the best options for experienced freelancers. They rank amongst the top paying in the industry.

8. Set Boundaries

Working online comes with a lot of schedule freedom. You are likely to overwork or underwork. If you are greatly motivated, you might work for longer hours. If you need external motivation, getting into a routine may be hard for you.

Think about your lifestyle as a mum. Do you have to take care of house chores? When are your most productive hours? You are in control of your time.

9. Get an Ideal Work Location

If you are likely to get tempted to check on the kids or try out a new recipe, working from home is not advisable. Get a workspace designed only for work. It does not have to be an office, but somewhere you can shut out all distractions.

10. Stick with it

Working online has its highs and lows. There is too much work at certain periods, and at other times, it's dead slow. It takes time to build a client base. However, if you do good work continuously, you can be sure of a steady workflow from your clients.

10 Habits That Hold You Back from Achieving Your Dream of Working Online and How to Stop Them

Patterns make up the foundation of our day-to-day lives. We have to build upon our daily practices, before paving the way for our routines and habits to shape us.

As such, we can either build ideal habits that will support us as we advance toward achieving our objectives or create bad habits that end up undermining us. Bad habits make it harder for us to succeed and achieve our set goals.

The one certain thing is that achieving your dreams is not an easy feat, particularly if you already have a set of bad habits. The following are ten bad habits holding you back from attaining your goals:

1. **Seeking approval**

If you place too much emphasis on what others think, it means that you have stopped listening to yourself. Attempting to gain the approval of others only serves to hold you back. There are instances when you should seek out other people's opinions, but this does not mean that you should look for accolades from all those closest to you.

You need to keep in mind that you are your own person. You have your failures and successes. A time will come when you will need to stand on your own.

2. **The need to always be perfect**

You need to remember that no single person is perfect. Constantly seeking perfection will work against you as you continue to unattainable bars. Every individual has things they are good at and others where they will struggle.

There are instances when you will fly, and other times when you will find yourself faltering. Rather than set expectations you cannot attain, you need to admit the fact that you have made some mistakes.

Make it a point to learn from your mistakes, and you will continue to grow stronger.

3. **Shifting the blame**

It is natural for you to want to shift the blame from yourself. Attributing your shortcomings to others occurs naturally to some people.

But rather than come up with excuses, you should strive to start taking action. Do not look for reasons why what has transpired is not your fault.

Instead, try to look at what you can to make amends. Keep in mind that you always have control over your actions, regardless of the circumstances facing you.

4. **Staying in your comfort zone**

Many people are averse to taking risks. After all, leaving your comfort zone requires you to take chances and take a leap of faith. This means that there is a chance that you may end up failing.

However, you will never really know what you can do if you refuse to try. It is possible that you will fail at some point, but this should not deter you from trying.

Push yourself to want more, and it will eventually happen for you.

5. Undefined goals

Everyone has a dream, concept, or idea that they would like to see transform into something real. But if you do not have a flawless vision and concrete plan, all this will mean nothing.

You need to define your goals before anything can start happening. You have to create a roadmap that will act as your guide.

It is easy for you to go off-course when you do not have a plan that can help pull you into the future. Create a plan from the get-go and stick to it.

6. Constantly putting yourself and others down

Putting others down or constantly engaging in negative talk does not do any good for your future. Telling others or yourself that 'you can't do anything right,' or 'you are stupid,' means that you are inviting negativity into your life.

By doing this, you are inflicting personal wounds that will only serve to haunt you. You have to put an end to these put-downs. Have a conversation with yourself and tell your inner self to get rid of your negative persona.

Try and replace all the negative habits you have developed with more positive ones. You should not place all your focus on what is going wrong, but rather, you should focus on what you have achieved.

7. Neglecting your well-being

Do not allow yourself to fall into habits that may harm your health, e.g., not getting enough sleep, not exercising enough, and eating poorly.

Bad health habits can negatively affect your physical and mental health. They will make you feel stressed and physically exhausted, and will increase your chances of developing an illness.

Such habits can affect your body's ability to perform. Make sure you have some personal time. Do not take life too seriously such that you end up missing out on what it has to offer.

8. Feeding distractions

The truth is that life is filled with all kinds of distractions. Social media, for instance, provides a lot of distractions.

When faced with many distractions, it becomes harder for you to focus your energy, thoughts, and strengths on your objectives.

Living a life filled with distractions means that your goals will not receive the attention they need. Try to slow things down to a manageable pace.

9. Inaction

Stop procrastinating if you want to achieve your goals. Do not get suckered into complacency and inaction by the various distractions in your life.

You will end up getting stagnated when you stop moving forward. Indifference and inertia will take over when you become reluctant to take that next crucial step.

A time will come when you will need to start doing and stop planning. Leaders need to seize opportunities whenever they arise.

10. Self-Doubt

Nothing kills dreams faster than self-doubt. The fear of rejection coupled with negative thinking only helps to fuel indecision and uncertainty.

Constantly questioning your goals and doubting your abilities only helps to fuel pessimistic thoughts. Holding yourself back will eventually contribute to your failure.

You will succeed when you start believing in yourself and get rid of the negative thoughts clouding your judgment.

You deserve to attain success at something. But the reality is that you may never achieve success if you keep letting your bad habits control your life. The bad habits discussed above are easy to avoid. The sooner you do this, the sooner you will start succeeding.

20 Ways to Improve Your Earning Potential

Remote workers are often constantly looking for new jobs and clients since most of the work is temporary. You can look for a part time or full time remote job to reduce the constant need to look for freelance work. Here are some actionable tips to improve your earning potential while working online.

1. **Find reliable remote jobs**

Knowing the right place to connect with remote employers will help you land more gigs. Traditional sites might not help you much as they are not exactly designed for remote workers. However, some sites, such as Remote.com or RemoteOK are other sites with location-flexible employers.

2. **Go out there and network**

Making connections with business owners and gig workers in your area can help you land some work online. Participate in networking events and join entrepreneurs' and freelancers' meetup groups.

3. **Develop the important traits of working online**

There are traits that are considered important by hiring managers. Can you adapt to the various working cultures and communicate effectively? Here are some traits that can improve your online earnings:

- Flexible
- Adaptive
- Trainable
- Proactive
- Self-starter
- Clear communicator
- Take constructive criticism

4. **Learn new skills**

Is your skill set lacking? This can be one of the reasons you get turned down for work. Enroll in a class you feel can help you get enough work. Take part in training that can make your portfolio much better.

Check the job descriptions of your desired jobs to understand the skills and experience required, then take up courses on platforms such as Skillshare, Udemy, Coursera, or LinkedIn Learning to improve on them.

5. **Take the part-time contracts**

Do not just give up if you do not get full-time gigs. You can still make a significant income by lining up a couple of part-time contracts. You might even discover you prefer diverse work. Part-time jobs will not only keep you busy but also help you stack up some cash.

6. **Create your remote worker's resume**

Business owners mostly look for different characteristics and skills in remote workers than in regular employees. Your resume should, therefore, highlight the experience and skills of a freelancer or gig worker. If you still use your regular office-work resume, you need to make an update.

7. **Familiarize yourself with online tools**

Each company has its own requirements in communications, online meetings, etc. You need to meet the various requirements to meet the demands of potential clients and employers. While one client prefers to use Skype or Zoom, another one is dedicated to WebEx. Don't be basic. Familiarize yourself with more tools to land more gigs.

8. **Build your online presence**

You have better chances to get hired if people know you. Create a likable online presence for people to seek you out. Establish social media accounts and create a professional website.

Feature your talents, accomplishments, and a portfolio of any relevant information to potential clients.

9. Ask for recommendations and referrals

When you are confident about your services, don't be afraid to use this to your own advantage. Ask your clients for referrals. Would they write a testimonial to add to your website? When you send out emails, include a link for clients to review your work.

10. Be a thought leader

Use your online presence to provide mentorship, trustworthy information, and predictions about your industry. Thought leaders have higher chances of excelling in their field. The names tend to appear when employers conduct searches related to their industry. Work on your brand to earn name recognition.

11. Ask for feedback

If you are constantly struggling to land gigs, you might not be doing something right. In most cases, clients will not utter a word if you turn them off; they just stop using your services. Even worse, they could warn others about your negative aspects.

Ask your clients about your performance. You will know what to change. It could be the quality of your work, your ability to meet deadlines or even your communication style.

12. Utilize fully seasonal work

Sports championships, conferences, holidays, and events are business boosters. Take advantage of the events to generate more money.

During these periods, businesses need more social media management, marketing, customer support, and web design. Simply engage in well-timed promotion and marketing.

13. Reach out to your old clients

Email lists are a gold mine. Periodically reconnect with clients you worked for earlier. They will have you in mind when your services are needed. Even better, some will recommend you to their connections.

14. **Learn to say no**

If you take every job that comes your way, you are likely to miss better opportunities. Don't take on a job because of desperation and fear. Being selective can be helpful in the long run.

15. **Invest time every day in client acquisition and business growth**

Even in those busy days, spare some time to network, reach out to clients, and market yourself. You won't get new clients if you don't set aside time for client acquisition

16. **Keep your paperwork simple**

Utilize automotive administration. The time you would otherwise spend with contracts, paperwork, financials, and filing will be spent on more resourceful things. There are many apps to help you forego the paperwork. You could even delegate the work to outside help.

17. **Partner with people who work online**

It is not fun turning down a lucrative job because you cannot meet the deadline or lack a certain skill. Reach out to someone who can help you get the job done. It is better to split the job than lose it. You can earn more by outsourcing to other freelancers.

18. **Know how to write a good pitch**

A cold pitch has the power to create a position that never existed. Some business owners do not realize the benefits of your services. An amazing pitch will help them see the significance of your services to their business.

19. **Consider in-house work for a certain period**

Sometimes, you may be required to spend some time learning a skill or working on a certain project at a desk which might eventually improve your marketability. You can always discuss a better work arrangement with the management. Perfecting a certain skill can give you the power to turn your employer into a client.

20. Consider local jobs

Working online doesn't entirely mean the global or national level. Do not limit yourself to major corporations or tech startups. There might be potential remote employers in your area. Some are not able to hire a full-time employee for bookkeeping, web design, or marketing. Your skills could be valuable to them.

Top 8 Secrets of Successful People Who Work Online

You need to adopt the habits of successful online income earners to make it work for you. These are the necessary habits that will get you started and keep you moving up the earnings ladder.

1. **Never stop learning**

Just like any career, working online requires you to keep reading to improve your knowledge. Have the thirst for learning and you'll be among the top crop of online success stories. Read blogs, and articles and enroll for courses.

Get as much information as possible and apply those that make sense. Find top blogs in your niche and subscribe. Have a hunger for knowledge and keep improving yourself. This will make you unstoppable.

2. **Take action: start small. Just start**

Dreamers are just that: dreamers with no actions. Once you have decided on what you'll do, get started with whatever you have and build from there. You have to get started for you to achieve the immense success ahead of you.

Start now. Start today. Stop procrastinating. There are only a few tomorrows. We don't know when the axe will fall on us. Take action now in the direction that you want to go. Whether you want to be a blogger or writer, what will make your dreams come true is to start. Start small, don't just stay there.

3. **Take it seriously, like you would a real job**

Just because you can work in your pajamas doesn't mean it is not a real job. You must treat it as such if you want to earn a living. There is competition just like there is for any job. You need to set yourself apart from the park.

Be professional. Type your cover letters and cold emails with professional language. Use proper grammar and use complete sentences, not shortcuts. Double check your work before you send

4. Be consistent

Starting is not enough. You have to make a decision every single day to do what you need to do not just to keep you afloat but to move forward, to improve yourself. Deliver high-quality work every time. Write blog posts to your blog consistently.

Consistent action toward your goal will bring immense success. Be consistent in marketing yourself. Upload new posts on your blog, connect with other writers on the forums, and use LinkedIn publisher and social media to advertise your work.

5. Have an action plan

Plan what you want to achieve in a month, in 6 months, in one year, or in five years. You need to know what you want, why you want it, and what you need to do to get what you want.

Working without a goal will make you settle for less, do less, and earn less. Have a definite amount of money you want to earn. Keep a goals journal and write your goals every day. Then keep improving your skills to make you better. Redesign your site, rewrite, rewrite your bio. Don't get stuck. Do all it takes to achieve your goals

6. Niche down

While it's good to taste the waters and try out many methods of working online, it is good to first select one and perfect it. Figure out what is best suited for you. What can you offer? If you're creative, writing or graphic design is best for you. Whatever you choose there is space for more writers to thrive. You just have to find your angle.

Choose one of the ways, say writing. Read as much as you can on that, then work on it. Later on, you can niche down to the topics that you want. For instance;

- Health writer
- Finance writer
- Home improvement writer
- Ebook writer

It is easier for clients to hire an expert in a niche than a general writer

7. Have a blog

Having a blog is a necessity for freelancers. It helps you to build your brand and for you to stand out. You can blog about what you do and share your experiences. Then, build your portfolio through your website. This sets you apart from many other freelancers. Market yourself to your clients and lead the traffic to your site from social media and LinkedIn.

8. Believe in yourself

Have confidence in your skills and you have what it takes to earn. You need confidence to ask for a higher rate. You need confidence to submit your pitches to websites. You need to believe that you have the skills.

Learn as much as you can to improve yourself. The internet has a lot of resources to help you learn anything you want to. YouTube has millions of videos. There is a wealth of information on Google, you just need to find courses, and blogs. Improve yourself and build your confidence.

Chapter 3: 50 Smart Ways to Make Money Online for Beginners

You have probably read different ways to make money but had to extract your money rather than earn it, there are ways to earn a living online that are mostly straightforward. They mostly demand that you learn skills to help you make a career out of what you do.

You need to devote the energy and time needed to get started and the grit to stick with it even when it seems slow when you start out.

Check out the resources on each way to make money in the form of links to get more information about how to get started.

Here are 50 legit ways to make money online you can consider:

1. **Become a Freelancer**

Freelancing is suitable for people who prefer to work at home or at any time they want anywhere. You can provide any skills you have such as writing, bookkeeping, calendar management or graphic design.

Upwork, People per Hour, and Freelancer are top freelance websites. You will need to create a freelancer profile to post the skill you are selling and provide appropriate details about your abilities and experience to get hired.

2. **Writing Articles on Authority Websites**

Many authority sites are always in search of fresh ideas and content to broaden their client base for maximum profits. Even though they already have content research and editorial teams, they are constantly finding new people with different ideas who can write articles.

To get started, find your topics of interest and write an informative article. Find an authority site in the industry related to your niche and contact them. Listverse.com, Blog.teamtreehouse.com, and photoshop tutorials.ws are some examples of amazing authority websites.

3. **Become a Ghostwriter**

A ghostwriter writes articles or ebooks for other individuals/companies. The person who hires you owns the completed work. To get started, apply for ghostwriting jobs on sites such as Fiverr, Upwork, Indeed, and People per hour.

4. **Sell your Service on Fiverr**

Fiverr, an online marketplace that offers services, products, and tasks. From digital marketing, graphics, and design, and advertising to music and audio, you can offer any service that people would be interested in. All you need to get started is to find your best skill, sign up, and create a gig on Fiverr.

5. **Start a blog**

Blogging is among the easiest ways to make money online. If you enjoy writing and have expertise in a certain area, you should consider sharing it with the world. However, it takes some time before a blog starts to make money for you.

It takes one to two days for a basic blog set up. Like a relationship, you should be committed for your blog to flourish. You will need to buy a domain name and get hosting. Get a domain name and affordable hosting package from Namecheap for just $28.88 per year. Click here to get started.

Owning a blog is a full time working online gig and also a chance to showcase your experience and services. You will need to be patient and dedicated to post regular content and push traffic to the blog. You can earn from the blog through selling ad space or sell your own products such as ebooks, courses or physical products.

6. **Sell Quote Printables**

Quote printables are simple quotes written on uniquely designed canvas using compelling fonts which are printable. With the availability of numerous photo editing tools, designing quote printables is quite easy.

If you possess the creative imagination to create and design printables you should consider selling quote printables. You can promote your products through social media, networking, blogging, and guest posting.

You will need tools like Canva, Adobe, or Photoshop. Canva is the easiest tool for beginners. Register with your email and start designing using the millions of templates available on the platform. Try Canva Pro free trial here.

7. **Creating Niche Websites**

A niche website focuses on a particular topic. If you are well informed on a specific topic in a large domain such as; in a domain like meditation, you can choose 'Meditation to reduce stress,' and you can create a niche website.

Create good quality content for the niche targeted audience and use affiliate programs to offer products related to the particular niche. Some affiliate programs include Amazon Associates, Commission Junction and Share a Sale.

You will need to buy a domain name and get hosting. Get a domain name and affordable hosting package from Namecheap for just $28.88 per year. Click here to get started.

8. **Become a Proofreader**

Get paid to carefully examine text to correct grammar, typing errors, spelling mistakes, and style. To be a proofreader, you should be native-like fluent in both written and spoken English, and have excellent comprehension and editing skills.

You also need to be familiar with different formatting styles, such as the MLA, Chicago Manual of Style, and the AP Style, to meet your client's requirements. Additional knowledge of word processing programs such as Microsoft Word or Google Docs is beneficial. You can also take proofreading courses.

Applying for the proofreader post on websites is a good way to get started. Some of the websites include:

- Proofreadingservices.com
- Scribendi.com
- Domainite.com

9. Start a Dropshipping Business

If you have very little start-up capital, dropshipping might be your fit. You don't have to worry about inventory, stock, shipping, packing, or handling. All you need is to create an online store and make sales for a profit.

Shopify.com is a simple way to start up. The website provides everything technical that you need to set your online store up including design, hosting, themes, domain name, and payment getaways.

10. Pinterest Marketing

Most online businesses and companies focus on marketing their products on other social media channels ignoring Pinterest. With over 100 million active users, Pinterest is a powerful platform for making money. 71% of Pinterest users are women, so if your products are relevant to female clients, you can reach your target market with less effort. To get started:

- Set clear goals
- Create your profile
- Post regularly
- Use relevant tags
- Write detailed comments
- Interact with the audience

You can use Pinterest to market your products or services or work as a Pinterest virtual assistant and help manage the accounts of different businesses.

11. Become a Social Media Evaluator

You probably spend some time each day checking various social media channels. It is possible to use this time to earn some money online.

Brands use social media campaigns to market products, improve user engagement and maintain an online presence. They hire social media evaluators to do these things. Applying for the social media evaluator post on Appen.com is a good starting point.

12. **Start Data Entry Work**

A data entry job typically involves reading and typing data from one source to another. You need basic computer skills, fast typing skills, a computer and internet access. There are many data entry scams on the internet today, so you should be cautious before signing up for any program. Legitimate data entry sites include:

- Hiresine.com
- Diondatasolutions.net
- Axiondata.com

13. **Sell Crafts and Art on Etsy**

If you are an artistic or crafty person who envisions, creates, and designs your own products/items, Etsy is a great option for you. The online seller and buyer community are similar to eBay, but Etsy focuses on selling handmade crafts, arts, or vintage items. Here's how to create your Etsy store:

- Decide on what to sell
- Choose your store name
- Set your store up
- Write a catchy description
- Use the right keywords and tags

Etsy is not available in some countries. You can instead learn how to make digital planners and sell them on your website or sell your services to Etsy store owners.

14. **Becoming an Amazon Associate**

If you love writing and explaining things in detail, you should definitely join the affiliate marketing program. You need to own a website or blog with daily traffic.

To become an Amazon associate, visit their site and sign up. If your website meets their standards, you will be approved within 5 days.

You will need to buy a domain name and get hosting. Get a domain name and affordable hosting package from Namecheap for just $28.88 per year. Click here to get started.

15. Reselling Items on eBay

eBay is the internet's most popular marketplace. From phones and handbags to books, you can list almost anything for sale. To be a successful eBay seller, you need a business-savvy mind and the know-how to get your items out there. To become a seller on eBay, sign up and be sure to have a PayPal account.

Ebay is not available in some countries. You can instead sell on other e-commerce stores in your countries such as Jumia.

16. Become a Virtual Call Centre agent

Virtual call center employees can work from anywhere. The agent receives a script with answers to possible questions. You need to be fluent in the particular operating language and have the ability to explain things on the phone. You can enroll in Working Solutions, and LiveOps to be an agent or set up a profile on Indeed.

17. Instagram Marketing

Do you love taking photos and using Instagram? You can grow your account to fetch you a significant income online. Over recent years, Instagram has gained popularity among brands due to its high number of active users. To get started you require:

- An Instagram account
- Appealing profile picture
- Impressive bio

Some of the best ways to monetize Instagram include:

- Affiliate marketing
- Sell your photos
- Create sponsored posts
- Sell your account
- Sell your products

18. Write Taglines and Slogans

Are you an avid thinker/reader who can use a few concise words to deliver a broad message? You can monetize that by writing taglines and slogans. If you are a beginner, here are some websites to visit for a clear picture:

- Idiomsite
- Sloganizer
- BrainyQuote

To participate in slogan writing contests, reputed websites to register to include:

- Upwork
- Sloganslingers
- Freelancer
- Simplyhired

19. Do Graphic Design

For businesses, graphic design is an important aspect. Graphics catch the consumer's eye and attract them to brands and products. A graphic designer designs logos, websites, product interfaces, illustrations, and print headers. 99designs.com, Coroflot.com, and inkd.com are some sites that offer graphic design jobs.

You will need tools like Canva, Adobe, or Photoshop. Canva is the easiest tool for beginners. Register with your email and start designing using the millions of templates available on the platform. Try Canva Pro free trial here.

20. Publishing a Kindle eBook

A Kindle eBook is a great source of consistent passive income. To publish a Kindle eBook, you need vast knowledge of a particular subject and the ability to explain in words that are easily understood. Amazon.com is highly recommended for eBook sales.

21. Do Interview Transcribing

An interview transcriber listens to a video or an audio interview and then converts it into writing. If you are able to understand different accents and can type fast, the job suits you well. Scribie.com, GoTranscript, Transcribe Me and Ubiqus are good sites with available transcription jobs. You can also create an Upwork profile and start selling transcription services.

22. Sell video course on Udemy.com

From programming to photography, Udemy features a large collection of courses. The course can be audio, text, or video. If you are well-versed in a certain topic, you can teach and explain it to an audience. It is recommended to deliver most of your course (at least 80%) in a video as it is more engaging than audio and text.

Record your videos and edit them in Canva, Filmora, or Adobe Premiere Pro.

23. Create a Membership site

A membership website features exclusive content only available to members who sign up. Members pay a fee and can interact with one another. Membership websites are suitable for people who like interacting, leading, and guiding a community. You need to be well-informed on a particular domain and have the ability to generate helpful and new content.

You will need to buy a domain name and get hosting. Get a domain name and affordable hosting package from Namecheap for just $28.88 per year. Click here to get started.

24. Creating and Editing Videos

Videos are trending currently. With free online tools, you can combine pictures, audio, and text into a video for customers online. Video editing services are easy to sell. You can either approach business owners or use online forums such as Fiverr.

Record your videos and edit them in Canva, Filmora, or Adobe Premiere Pro.

25. Starting a YouTube Channel

Starting your own YouTube Channel is a simple money maker and requires little or no investment. You can record videos using a camcorder or even your phone. Even better, it takes just a few minutes to start a YouTube channel. The more videos you get, the more money you earn. It is important to maintain uniqueness and engage your viewers.

Record your videos and edit them in Canva, Filmora, or Adobe Premiere Pro. Here is a free video editing course to try out. You can also check Udemy for paid video editing courses.

26. Start Copywriting

Copywriting simply means writing copy to market or advertise. The copy should persuade potential clients to buy products. You might need to learn some concepts of psychology to be a successful copywriter. Iwriter and Upwork are some good websites where copywriters can get jobs.

27. Join Appen.com

The US-based company offers remote jobs globally. You only require a laptop and a good internet connection. To get hired, fill out an application form online and then upload your resume. If you make it to the shortlist, you have to take a three-part exam to qualify. You can only attempt the exam twice. Appen pays about $13/per hour to US citizens and $7/hour to African/Asian country citizens.

28. Sell Private Label Rights (PLR)

PLR provides an opportunity to make quick money without taking time to create a good product. PLR is a license the product creator offers to give you the right to use the product anyhow including reselling the product at your own price. Theplrstore, Bigcontentsearch, and Master-resale-rights are some online marketplaces to get PLR products.

29. Do Affiliate Marketing

Affiliate marketing is based on commission per product bought by customers brought by affiliate marketing efforts. Affiliate marketing is suitable for people who like to write, explain, talk, and are persuasive.

To start, choose a product, from a domain you are conversant with, that pays a commission when you make a sale through your affiliate link. You can find products on sites like Sharesale.com, Clickbank.com, and Jvzoo.com.

You will need to create a blog to post content and link your affiliate links. You can also advertise the links on social media platforms such as Pinterest and Instagram if you have a large following.

Get a domain name and affordable hosting package from Namecheap for just $28.88 per year. Click here to get started.

30. Becoming an Online Tutor

Today's busy lifestyle has resulted in people opting for online coaching due to its convenience. If you have completed a study in a particular subject or hold a college degree, you qualify to be an online tutor. For a start, sign up for online tutoring sites Studypoint.com and Tutor.com are reputable online tutoring sites.

31. Doing Document Translation

Global businesses need to communicate in a language their customer understands. They need multilingual people to effectively convert written documents from one language to another. If you speak 2 or more languages and love to write, you should give document translation a try.

To get started, upload your resume on Translatorscafe.com and list your services and rates. Gengo.com and Lingosaur.com also provide translation jobs.

32. Becoming a Research Assistant

A research assistant is hired to carry out research, collect data, and neatly present it. The job requires strong analytical skills, good grammar, and problem-solving skills. To get started, submit your application at Askwonder.com, or Justanswer.com.

33. Become a Social Media Manager

Most brands and companies own several social media accounts. As their client base broadens, it is difficult to engage with the customers. A social media moderator is hired to monitor social media channels and also make sure user-generated content is appropriate.

If you have a Facebook, Instagram, Twitter or Tiktok account, you can be paid to use social media instead of social media using you. As a social media manager you will write and publish posts for companies. You will need to be conversant with the platforms and have basic photo and video editing skills and also graphic design and copywriting skills to create captivating and engaging posts.

To get started, learn about the different social media channels, build your social media presence, and apply for social media manager jobs on freelancing websites.

34. Do Voice Acting (Voice Overs)

Voice acting involves providing voices that represent a character such as cartoon characters. If you are good at mimicry or have a compelling voice, voice acting can get you an income. This is an in demand skill needed by movie directors, animators and other media production companies.

Websites such as Voicebunny and voice123.com that offer voice acting jobs. You can also set up a professional profile on different freelancing websites and apply for jobs.

35. Sell products or services online

First, you need to identify a market and determine what products or services you can offer. Next, you need to create a website or online store to showcase your products or services. This involves selecting a domain name, building a website or storefront, and setting up payment options.

Once your website is up and running, you need to focus on marketing and promoting your business through social media, email marketing, and other online channels. It's also important to track your performance and make adjustments to your business strategy as needed. Finally, make sure to comply with any relevant regulations and laws related to online businesses in your region.

You will need to buy a domain name and get hosting. Get a domain name and affordable hosting package from Namecheap for just $28.88 per year. Click here to get started. You can also use a Shopify store instead of Woocommerce on WordPress.

36. **Join Q&A Sites**

Sometimes our personalized questions remain unanswered by search engines. Q&A sites offer quick personal answers to problems. Are you an expert in a particular field? Make a dime by answering people's questions online. You don't need new skills or start-up capital to start. JustAnswer.com and Askwonder.com are some of the best Q&A sites.

37. **Starting your Book Review Store**

Publish reviews about books. If you are passionate about reading, make some money out of it. Start a website and write honest reviews for the books. You can also become an Amazon affiliate by promoting books using Amazon affiliate links.

38. **Click and Sell photos**

If you love to take pictures that are creative and versatile, you can turn your skill into a job. Here are some websites you should join to sell your photography: SmugMug.com, iStockPhoto.com, and GettyImages.com.

39. **Get Paid to Tweet**

If you are a frequent Twitter user, you can make money by posting 'Sponsored tweets.' Earnings rely on the number of followers you have. You don't need any technical setup or money to start. Approach network marketing companies in your state or sign up on Sponsoredtweets.com to find sponsors.

40. **Do Email Marketing**

Email marketing involves using your email list of your blog subscribers to market certain products. Building an email list takes time. Using a free email course or eBook is a great way to add to your email list. To make money, send your affiliate product links and promotional emails to the email list regularly

41. **Become a Captioner**

Captioning is the conversion of the audio content of a video into text. Subtitles on television series and movies are usually typed by captioners. A captioner should be able to understand multiple accents in the operating language. To get started you need a computer, a good internet connection, and a headset. You can work as a captioner on Rev, HappyScribe, or Take1.

42. **Sell Products on Zazzle**

Zazzle has millions of customizable products that are made to order. Users can print drawings, designs, or photos on various items. With numerous tools like photoshop, it is easy to convert designs to digital format. Create and refine your digital design sign up at Zazzle.com. Set up your shop and start selling your designs. Zazzle handles shipping, printing, and payment processing.

43. **Start Your Podcast**

A podcast is a digital audio file available on the web to download. New installments are automatically received by subscribers. If you like to explain things in depth, and are persuasive, starting your podcast is one of your options to make money online. Ensure your podcast is compelling to make sales. Inserting a commercial in the podcast is another way to earn money.

44. **Doing Smartphone Photography**

You can simply make money by clicking photos on your phone to sell. Some apps give photography assignments that need you to upload pictures using the app. You have to make sure the pictures look professional. Clashot, and Zoomer, are some apps that pay you for your photography.

45. Do Facebook Marketing

Promote a product on Facebook to earn money. You can start Facebook marketing by creating a page on Facebook to promote products or promotional posts. Get more traffic to your page by using Facebook ads to get more people to buy products through your affiliate link.

46. Join Focus Groups

A focus group gives opinions and advice about a service, product, concept, or advertisement. Focus groups are almost similar to surveys but you need in-depth knowledge about the relevant subject. You need to take part in discussions or use a video recording to share your insights. FocusGroup and ResearchNichols are groups you can participate in. Get more sites here.

47. Joining Micro Job Sites

Micro job sites pay you to complete micro-tasks. The micro jobs can include calculating the bill amount, counting items on a shopping list, or commenting on a blog. Micro jobs do not pay much per task but can fetch you money if you have some free time. To get started, sign up at mTurk.com, OneSpace.com, or these sites and earn some money.

48. Sell Print on Demand Products

Spring (formerly TeeSpring) is a great way to make and sell designer apparel online. You simply get paid to produce your design. If you have a ready design, then you can create a spring campaign in minutes. You have to promote your T-shirt using paid ads or on social media. If you have a large following on social media, you can make a high income from spring campaigns.

- Find a niche or target audience
- Research T-Shirt Ideas that relate to your target audience.
- Design the T-Shirt on Canva or hire a graphic designer on Fiverr or Upwork
- Upload to Spring and market on social media. Use Ads to increase your earning. Once a customer buys, Spring will print and sell the t-shirts.

You can also design t-shirts and sell them to your local customers

49. Share Links on Social Media

Social media marketing has gained popularity today. Businesses need people to help them promote their services or products on social media channels. If your social media following is large, you can make a substantial income by sharing links with your followers. Check out Viraliti.com or Rakuten to get started.

You can also become an Amazon or Jumia affiliate and get paid to share links on the internet. Use your special links to products and share them online.

50. Buy and Sell Domain Names

The website address you key in on the browser's address bar is a domain name E.g. Facebook.com. There are domain names with a commercial value that have the potential to increase in demand with time. You can get a domain name for about $6 on Namecheap.com. List the domain name for sale on websites at a higher price. Sedo is an excellent marketplace for domain names.

Chapter 4: BONUS

In the last chapter you've learned the 50 legit ways to earn a living online. Choose one that piques your interest then get started. Don't attempt too many ideas at the same time. Once you get success with one, you can always move on to the next one.

This bonus chapter shares 20 best job jobs to find online and remote jobs. We also share 60 frequently asked questions about working online.

Bonus 1: 20 Best Job Boards to Find Remote Work

1. Upwork - This is one of the best platforms to find freelance work. It helps you connect with clients from different parts of the world for various jobs such as writing, web development, design and social media management.
2. Freelancer - It offers a global platform for freelancers from different parts of the world. You can get all types of jobs such as programming, video editing and design.
3. Fiverr - Freelancers can offer their services in the form of gigs in different categories such as ghostwriting, web design and logo design. There are many other gigs that you can offer like meal plans, coaching among others.
4. Remote.co - You can get remote work for different careers such as writing, web design and customer service.
5. We Work Remotely - You will also get different remote jobs opportunities from web development to project management and customer support.
6. FlexJobs - The job board features curated remote and flexible job opportunities, including writing, marketing, and customer service.
7. Virtual Vocations - The job board has remote jobs such as writing, graphic design, and web development.
8. Remote OK - The job board has jobs in tech, marketing, and design.
9. Jobspresso - Here you will get remote jobs in various fields, including writing, marketing, and customer service.
10. Working Nomads - This job board features remote job opportunities from writing to software development.

11. Indeed - The job search engine that allows you to filter job postings by location, including remote work opportunities.
12. LinkedIn - LinkedIn is a professional networking site that allows you to search for remote job opportunities in various fields.
13. Guru - This is also a freelance platform that allows businesses to hire freelancers for writing, design, and programming.
14. Remote.com - This job board has remote jobs in tech and marketing.
15. Outsourcely - The platform also offers writing, graphic design, and virtual assistant jobs.
16. Remotive- Here you will get writing, sales and marketing jobs among others.
17. SkipTheDrive - You'll also get writing, design, and customer service jobs.
18. Just Remote - Here you'll get writing, programming, and marketing jobs.
19. Dribbble - The job board features remote jobs in design and web development.
20. Pangian - The job board has remote jobs for writers, designers, and programmers.

Bonus 2: 60 FAQS About Working Online

Many people are apprehensive about working online due to the perception that there do not exist any real online work opportunities. But the one thing you should note is that for every one legit work-from-home assignment, you are likely to find sixty to seventy job scams.

As such, finding a good online job amidst all these scams can seem like a futile task. But with these tips, you should have a good starting point. The following list of 100 frequently asked questions about working online will help shed more light on work-from-home jobs:

1. What is remote work?

Remote work refers to any job or task that is completed over the internet, without the need for physical presence in an office or workplace.

2. What are some common types of online work?

Common types of online work include freelance writing, graphic design, web development, virtual assistance, and online tutoring.

3. What skills are needed for online work?

The skills needed for online work vary depending on the type of work, but generally include computer literacy, communication skills, and task-specific skills like writing, design, or coding.

4. How can I find remote work?

There are several websites and platforms that connect freelancers with remote work, including Upwork, Freelancer, and Fiverr.

5. What is freelancing?

Freelancing is a type of online work where a person provides services on a project-by-project basis to clients, rather than working for a single employer.

6. How do I become a freelancer?

A freelancer is a person who gets to choose tasks that they are best suited to do. It can be in web development, accounting, writing, or even programming. To become a freelancer, you need to identify your skills, create a portfolio of work, and start reaching out to potential clients.

7. How can I start working from home?

It is simple. All you need to do is find a good freelance website and register your details. Ensure you follow all the instructions, taking care not to leave out any details. Depending on the website you have signed up on, it should not take more than a few days to receive your approval/rejection email. If approved, you can start looking for work immediately. If rejected, keep trying until you get it right.

8. How do I find online jobs on sites like Upwork?

Look for work-from-home jobs based on your existing skill set and send in your application.

9. Can you work from anywhere?

Yes, there are thousands of online workers from across the globe working online.

10. I am looking for a good online job. How can I find one?

There exist thousands of remote or work-from-home available on many online job websites like Upwork, Fiverr, and Freelancer.com. You can also use job boards like flex jobs, Problogger and Blogging Pro to find remote jobs.

11. Can I use my cellphone to work?

Apart from the rare cases where you can use a tablet or cellphone to work, you need a laptop or desktop computer to work online.

12. How will I land my first online job if I do not possess any qualifications to work online?

We all have a starting point. Everyone starts at ZERO, regardless of whether working online or offline. Focus on the skills that you can offer to your clients

13. Is it possible to only work during the weekends?

Yes, this is possible. But keep in mind that job opportunities tend to be limited. Consider finding a stable online job where you can work for between twenty and forty hours each week.

14. Can I set my work schedule?

Yes, you can. You have an option when it comes to your work schedule and the clients you work for.

15. Are there online part-time jobs?

Yes, there are lots of part-time tasks available. You only need to find one that works best for you.

16. What is the secret to finding clients?

It is not as hard as you may have been told. Patience and a good strategy are key when starting.

17. How much money will I need to get started?

Freelancing websites such as Upwork and Fivver do not charge you anything to get started.

18. What are the benefits of remote work

Benefits of remote work include increased flexibility, reduced commute times, and the ability to work from anywhere with an internet connection.

19. What are some common challenges of remote work?

Common challenges of remote work include isolation, lack of structure, and difficulty separating work and personal life.

20. Who is a virtual assistant?

A virtual assistant is a remote worker who provides administrative, technical, or creative assistance to clients from a remote location.

21. How do I become an online tutor?

An online tutor is a remote worker who provides educational instruction to students over the internet. To become an online tutor, you typically need to have expertise in a specific subject area, as well as a teaching certification or degree.

22. What is an online course?

An online course is a digital learning experience that is completed over the internet, usually through a combination of video lectures, assignments, and assessments.

23. How do I create an online course?

To create an online course, you need to identify your area of expertise, develop a course curriculum, and create engaging video content and assignments.

24. What is affiliate marketing?

Affiliate marketing is a type of online marketing where a person earns a commission by promoting someone else's products or services.

25. How do I get started with affiliate marketing?

To get started with affiliate marketing, you need to identify a niche, find relevant products or services to promote, and start promoting them through your website or social media channels.

26. What is dropshipping?

Dropshipping is a type of e-commerce business where a person sells products online without keeping any inventory.

27. How does dropshipping work?

With dropshipping, the seller markets and sells products online, but the products are shipped directly from the supplier to the customer.

28. What is e-commerce?

E-commerce refers to the buying and selling of goods and services over the internet.

29. How can I start an ecommerce business

To start an ecommerce business, you need to identify a niche, source products, build an online store, and start marketing your products.

30. What is online content creation?

Online content creation refers to the creation of digital content like blog posts, videos, and social media posts.

31. What qualifications do I need to start working on online jobs?

The qualifications are in many cases set by the client. Look for tasks you are competent in.

32. Do I need a freelancer profile to work online?

Yes, this is a must-have. Create one on Upwork, Fiverr, or any other job board.

33. I have not linked my bank or PayPal to my account. Could it be the reason my Upwork profile was rejected?

I do not think so. The information you provide in your profile will act as the basis for the approval or rejection.

34. How will I know if my Upwork profile has been approved or rejected?

The website you have signed up on will send you an email.

35. My Upwork profile keeps getting rejected. What should I do?

Edit your current profile and ensure it is 100% complete and submit it again.

36. How do I get connects on Upwork to enable me to start applying for jobs?

Check around the website. Navigate to the settings page to check the requirements. You may need to log in a few times for this to happen.

37. When do I get new Connects on Upwork?

The connects are dependent on your billing cycle. They are refreshed at the start of each new cycle. But you can buy more connects any time you wish.

38. Do I need Payoneer or PayPal to join work from home websites?

Yes, you need to have a payment account to get paid. Set up a Paypal, Wise, or Payoneer account to get paid after you complete your work.

39. Do I need to provide a payment method every time I am hired?

You only need to provide a payment method once. The payments will then be sent to your chosen payment method.

40. How does bidding on freelance sites work?

You get to set a price for the services you are offering. Other freelancers can bid lower or higher than you.

41. I am looking for work online, but I do not know how to click the apply button.

If working on a bidding website, all you need to do is click the apply button, write a proposal, and click the submit button.

42. What does a project with a "fixed price "imply?

This means that the price of that task or project is non-negotiable.

43. How can I adjust my proposal terms from hourly to fixed rates?

You will be required to send a request to the client you are working for so that they can make the necessary adjustment on their side.

44. It is necessary for me to have a headset and camera when I do not have a client yet?

This is not necessary. It only applies when the client would like to interview before hiring you.

45. Do freelance websites allow the use of Skype or video interviews?

Websites tend to have different policies when it comes to client-worker interactions. Go through the terms and conditions on each platform to be sure.

46. What does it mean when the system says that the payment method is not verified?

It means that your client is yet to link their preferred payment details, e.g., cards or bank account. Ensure that the client's payment details are verified before you start working.

47. How can I check whether my client is verified on a bidding website?

Navigate to the link containing the original job offering and click on the client profile.

48. How do I go about setting the escrow payments?

Your client will be in charge of setting this up, not you. If you work with sites like Upwork, the system already has escrow payment protection.

49. How to get clients on bidding websites?

Ensure that you have good skills. You will also need to be diligent when applying for jobs.

50. How can I receive my payments if I do not have a bank account?

You will need to have an account like Payoneer or PayPal. You cannot withdraw your funds without an active account.

51. How often should I log into my freelancing account?

It depends on the number of tasks you are working on. You do not have to keep logging in if you do not have an ongoing task.

52. How should I address the client when sending in a proposal?

It is always best to try and establish the client's name. You can find this information on the jobs page.

53. How will I know whether the client has received my proposal or not?

You will receive an automatic notification when you send your proposal

54. Will, the client, hire me immediately or will I be interviewed?

This is dependent on the client. It may take a few days.

55. Is it okay if I am not truly fluent in English?

This should not be a big concern. The exception only applies when dealing with jobs that require English fluency.

56. The client is yet to respond to my messages, yet I have completed the tasks. What should I do?

Follow up with the client and then wait. For platforms such as Upwork, always work when the client has set up a paid milestone. The money is held on escrow and will be released once the client has reviewed the work.

57. Are all jobs worth the same amount of money?

No, it depends on the job involved and your current set of skills

58. A client wants me to work for less than $3/hour. Is this ok?

No, the minimum rate set by many freelance websites is about $5 per hour. Do not accept a lower offer. Although most beginners start with low pay, don't work for free.

59. Does the client need to make a down payment before I start working?

It all comes down to the discussions you had with the client in question. If you are working on platforms such as Upwork, you get escrow protection.

60. On average, how much can I earn from online jobs?

There is no average figure. It depends on your skills and the projects involved.

Conclusion

Thank you for reading the "Busy Mom's Guide to Working Online: 50 Legitimate Ways to Make Money Online."

It is the ultimate guide for anyone looking to make money from the comfort of their own home. The book has shared the basics of working online, the pros and cons of working online and what you need to get started.

Working online was a game changer for me when I had to quit my 9-5. I have been able to be there for my child and have the freedom to work when I want from wherever I am. I have worked with clients from all over the world, I have published books on Amazon and I currently run an online consultancy. So, I know that anything is possible as long as you put your mind, effort and time in it.

Don't be overwhelmed with the 50 ways to make money online. Choose one or two ways that are aligned to your skills and interests and are interconnected and take action. For example, if witing comes easy for you, you cna become a freelancer writer but also start a blog or publish ebooks on Amazon. The opportunities are unlimited. Be sure to use the resources shared in this book to get further reading and resources to get started.

It is time to turn your skills, talents and passion into a full tiem profitable online business. Start today the journey towards financial freedom! All the best!

P.S: Please remember to leave a review to help me reach to more readers who will benefit from this information.

Thank you,

Beatrice

www.ingramcontent.com/pod-product-compliance
Lightning Source LLC
Chambersburg PA
CBHW070414230526
45471CB00006B/2802